CO
GADGETS

SMALL Big facts BOOKS

PaRragon
Bath · New York · Singapore · Hong Kong · Cologne · Delhi · Melbourne

WHAT'S ON THE PAGE

The pages of this book are packed with super stats, fantastic facts and, of course, cool gadgets. Here's what you'll find on each page!

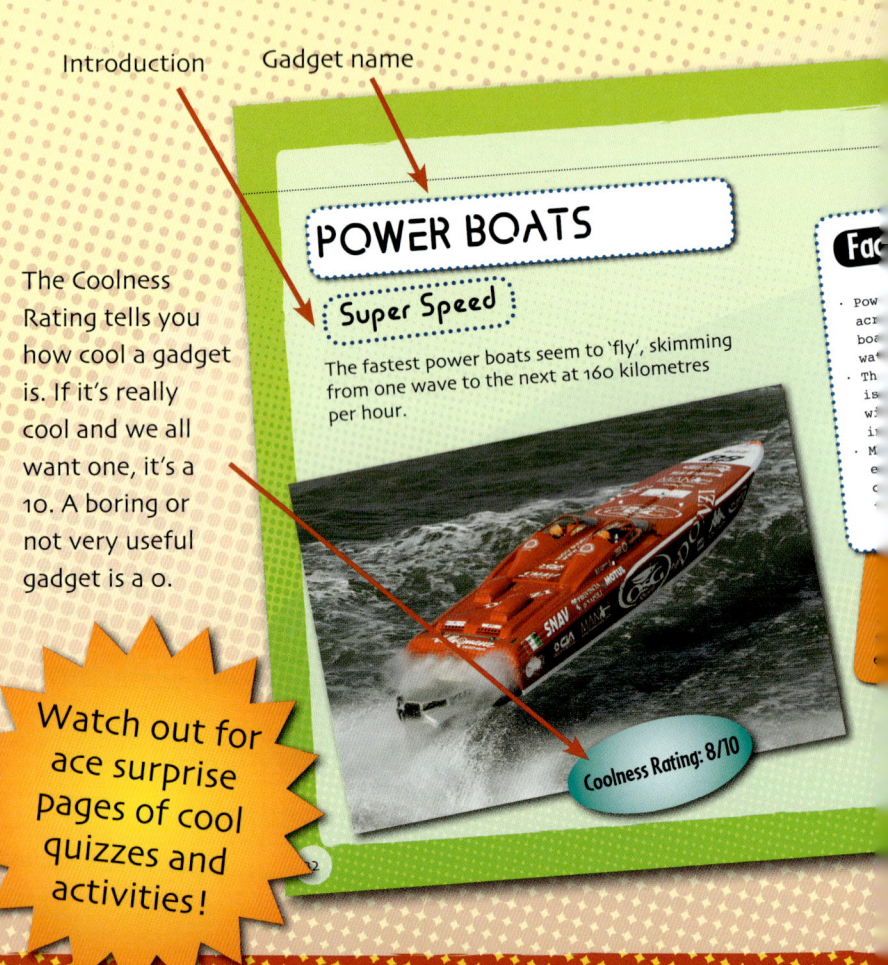

Introduction

Gadget name

The Coolness Rating tells you how cool a gadget is. If it's really cool and we all want one, it's a 10. A boring or not very useful gadget is a 0.

POWER BOATS

Super Speed

The fastest power boats seem to 'fly', skimming from one wave to the next at 160 kilometres per hour.

Coolness Rating: 8/10

Watch out for ace surprise pages of cool quizzes and activities!

4

The handy visual key at the top right of each page is a quick reference telling you what type of gadget you're looking at.

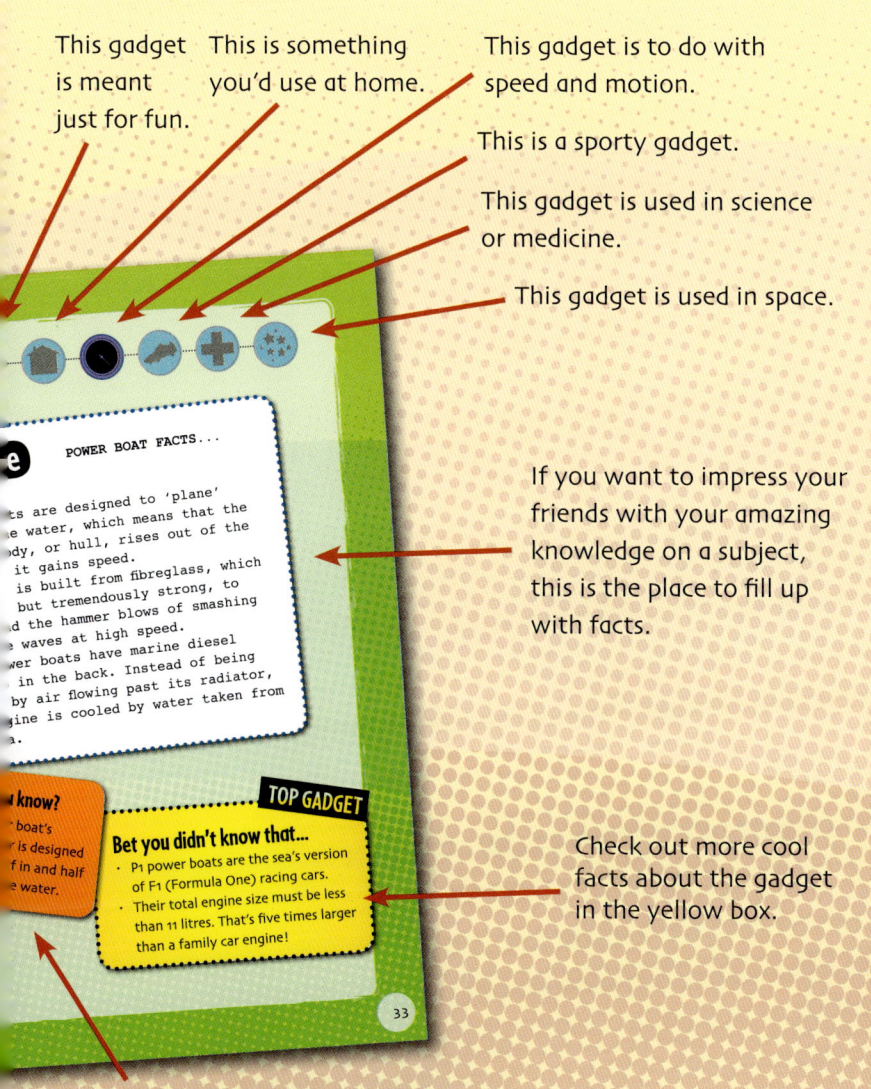

This gadget is meant just for fun.

This is something you'd use at home.

This gadget is to do with speed and motion.

This is a sporty gadget.

This gadget is used in science or medicine.

This gadget is used in space.

POWER BOAT FACTS...

...ts are designed to 'plane' ...e water, which means that the ...dy, or hull, rises out of the ...it gains speed.
...is built from fibreglass, which ...but tremendously strong, to ...d the hammer blows of smashing ...e waves at high speed.
...er boats have marine diesel ...in the back. Instead of being ...by air flowing past its radiator, ...gine is cooled by water taken from ...

If you want to impress your friends with your amazing knowledge on a subject, this is the place to fill up with facts.

...know?
...boat's
...is designed
...f in and half
...e water.

TOP GADGET

Bet you didn't know that...
- P1 power boats are the sea's version of F1 (Formula One) racing cars.
- Their total engine size must be less than 11 litres. That's five times larger than a family car engine!

Check out more cool facts about the gadget in the yellow box.

33

The orange box gives you more info about this gadget or a similar gadget.

5

AUDIO GADGETS

Music on the Move

Listening to music outside the home used to mean taking a bulky CD player – and if it got jogged it skipped. Now your tunes can be stored in a gadget as small as your finger.

Coolness Rating: 7/10

TOP GADGET

Bet you didn't know that...

- An MP4 watch stores music, video, photos and games.
- It has a flash memory, a small screen and plug-in headphones.
- It can also record sounds and tell the time!

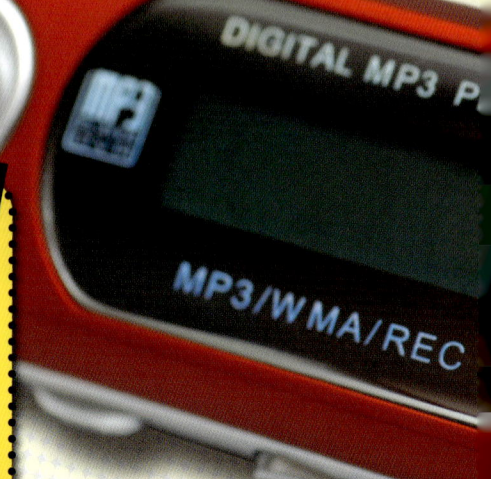

Fact File

MP3 FACTS...

- An MP3 docking station has a slot to plug in the player, which feeds the music into a powerful amplifier and loudspeakers. The MP3 player charges its battery while docked.
- The USB attachment plugs into the computer.
- One GB (gigabyte) of memory holds roughly 250 songs.
- MP3 players store sounds in two ways. Some use a flash drive, which is a memory microchip with no moving parts. Others use a tiny hard-disc drive, like the spinning magnetic disc in a computer's hard drive.

Did you know?

To get music on to a computer, songs are ripped from a CD (compact disc) into a compressed audio format.

GAMES CONSOLES

Play Away

A games console is an interactive entertainment computer connected to a video display. All you need is quick thinking – and fast fingers!

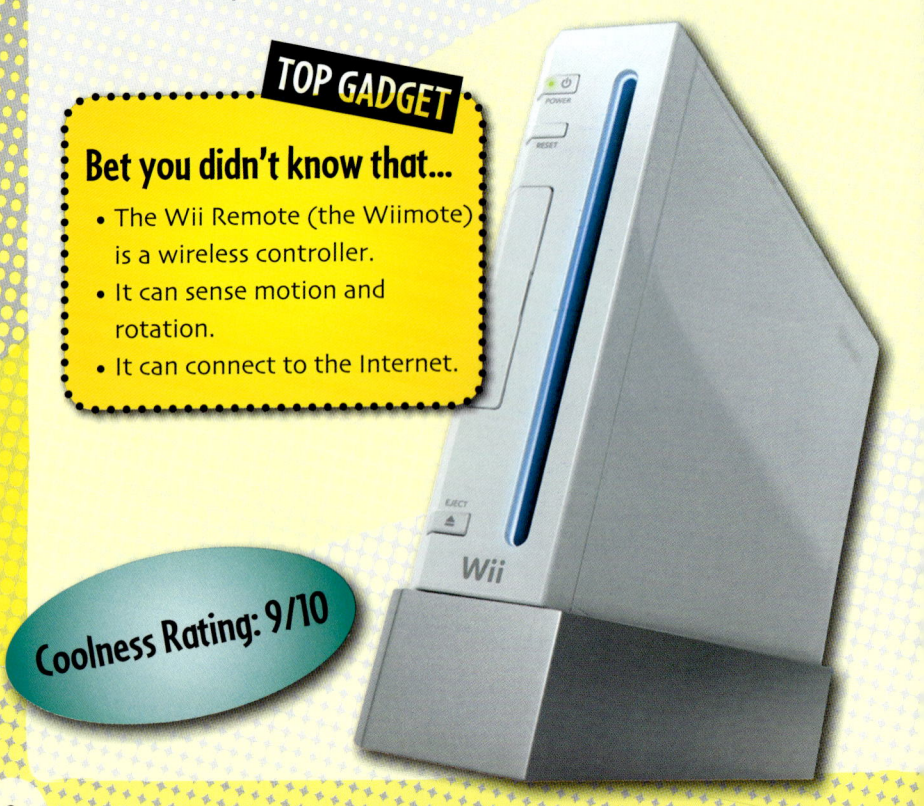

TOP GADGET

Bet you didn't know that...
- The Wii Remote (the Wiimote) is a wireless controller.
- It can sense motion and rotation.
- It can connect to the Internet.

Coolness Rating: 9/10

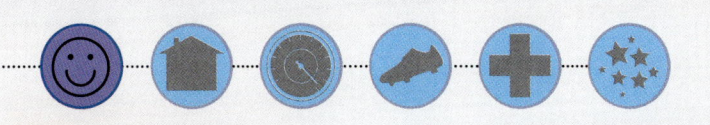

Did you know?

Making a computer game can take a team of graphic designers, animators, strategists and software specialists up to three years.

Fact File

GAMING FACTS...

- Donkey Kong is one of Nintendo's most successful games. It first appeared in 1981.
- The Xbox 360 is a '7th generation' system from Microsoft. You can use it to play against others on the Internet.
- Characters are made from 3-D shapes called polygons.
- Mini games can be played on mobile phones, MP4 watches, MP3 players and hand-held portable games consoles.
- Nintendo's DS Lite (DS means dual screen) has one ordinary screen and one touch-screen. A wireless link allows you to play with others nearby.

COOL CAMERAS

Stunning Snaps

With a digital camera, you can check the images on the camera's screen straight after shooting, dump the dud ones and make printed photos minutes later.

Coolness Rating: 6/10

Fact File — CAMERA FACTS...

- Light from the scene you want to photograph gets into the digital camera through the lens.
- The lens focuses light rays on to a microchip called a CCD (charge-coupled device).
- The CCD has millions of tiny pixels. The pixels turn the light rays into electronic signals. All the signals from all the pixels make up an electronic version of the scene.
- The camera's memory card stores the photos electronically on a set of microchips.

Did you know?

A 'high resolution' picture means more, smaller pixels, which makes the image more detailed.

TOP GADGET

Bet you didn't know that...

- An SLR (single lens reflex) camera is made up of a camera body plus a clip-on lens.
- A wide-angle lens is used to capture a big scene.
- A telephoto lens can take pictures of something that is far away.

TV AND CINEMA

Amazing Images

Today's sleek, flat, widescreen TVs can hang on the wall like a painting. The two main TV technologies are LCD (liquid crystal display) and plasma.

Fact File

TV FACTS...

- A flat screen reflects less light.
- An LCD screen contains millions of tiny crystals or pixels. Each has three sub-pixels of red, green and blue. These crystals 'twist' when electricity passes through them, to let through different amounts of light.
- Plasma screens also have pixels, but each pixel is made up of three tiny cells containing a special gas. When electricity passes through, the gas glows bright red, blue or green.
- HDTV (high-definition television) means the screen contains more, and tinier, pixels. This makes small details of the picture clearer.

Coolness Rating: 6/10

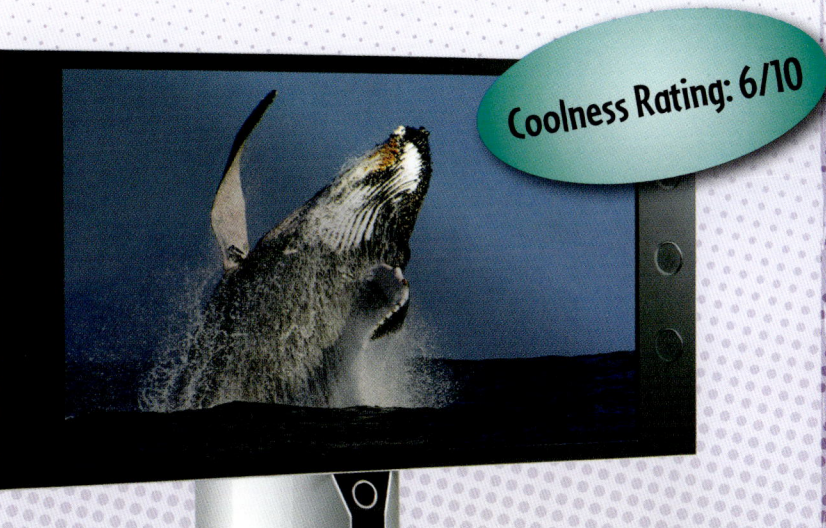

TOP GADGET

Bet you didn't know that...

IMAX ('Image Maximum') cinemas have 16-metre-high screens. IMAX movies are shot on special film that is ten times larger than normal film!

Did you know?

Most CD and DVD readers have a red laser, but Blu-ray and HD-DVD discs use a blue laser.

MOBILE PHONES

Cool Communication

Modern mobile phones include features such as camera, video with sound, MP3 music, games, television, email, visual voicemail and the Internet. (You can also talk on them!)

Did you know?
Mobile phone masts can be disguised as trees!

Fact File

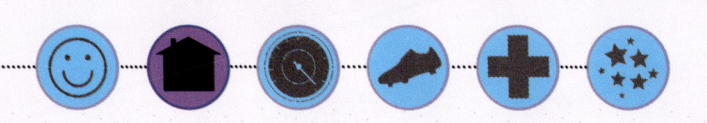

PHONE FACTS...

- When a text message or SMS (short message service) is sent, it travels as radio waves into the network via a mobile phone mast. The message is stored at an SMSC (short message service centre). The SMSC regularly checks the phone of the person you're sending the message to. When the phone is switched on, the SMSC forwards the text message.
- The BlackBerry is one of a range of palm-sized gadgets called PDAs (personal digital assistants). These are hand-held computers that work using digital wireless technology.
- PDA handsets link to a central control system. As well as being a mobile phone, they can receive and send emails.

TOP GADGET

Bet you didn't know that...
The Apple iPhone uses liquid crystal technology. You choose keys by pressing the large touch screen.

Coolness Rating: 8/10

LAPTOPS AND MEMORY DEVICES

Compact Computers

Coolness Rating: 7/10

TOP GADGET

Bet you didn't know that...
- The 2004 NASA supercomputer can do trillions of calculations per second.
- It helps work out how spacecraft will perform.
- It has 10,240 processors, 20 terabytes (20,000 GB) of RAM, 440 terabytes of storage and 10 petabytes (10 million GB) of archive storage!

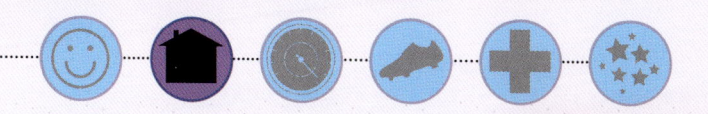

You can use a laptop anywhere – on the train, in the garden, even on the toilet! Modern laptops have no trailing cables to trip over.

Did you know?
The famous Swiss Army Knife now includes a memory stick.

Fact File

COMPUTER FACTS...

- The 'brain' of the laptop is the CPU (Central Processing Unit). It is actually several chips in one casing with rows of metal strips to connect it to other components.
- Laptops replace the mouse with a trackpad, a flat area where moving your finger moves the screen cursor.
- Bluetooth connects devices such as mobile phones and laptops directly to each other. Wi-Fi connects devices to networks such as the Internet.
- Computers and electronic gadgets need memory. Flash sticks are memory microchips protected in a casing. They are used for all kinds of data, including pictures and video.
- Memory cards fit into small devices such as digital cameras.

INTERNET AND WEBCAMS

Wireless World

The Internet allows computers, cameras and other devices around the world to be linked.

Coolness Rating: 9/10

Fact File

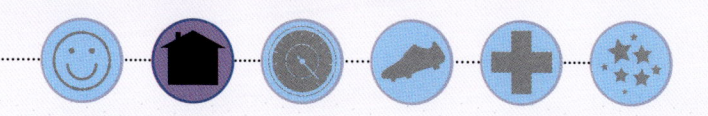

INTERNET FACTS...

- The Internet is organised in small and large groupings, from home computers in a village to those linked as a local area network (LAN), such as computers in a big company.
- Iceland has the highest national percentage of Internet users (86%).
- Link a digital camera with a microphone to the Internet, and you have a webcam! It can send pictures and sounds to anyone in an instant, even if they are on the other side of the world.
- Webcams are often used for security reasons, to watch banks, shops and even school playgrounds.

Did you know?

The first time a digital camera was linked to a computer network was to show scientists when their coffee was ready!

TOP GADGET

Bet you didn't know that...

The SOHO (Solar and Heliospheric Observatory) satellite takes pictures of the Sun. Its special cameras record images of sunspots and solar flares. Images are then uploaded to the Internet.

DIGITAL RADIO

Awesome Airwaves

For a long time, radio sounded crackly, but the invention of transistors, followed by DAB (Digital Audio Broadcasting), has transformed the sound of the radio.

Did you know?
Digital radio turns sound into a pattern of 0s and 1s, then uses thousands of on-off pulses per second to transmit the data.

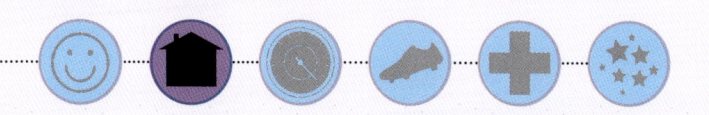

TOP GADGET

Bet you didn't know that...
- DAB information includes sounds, time and date, the radio station playing, its type of music and the latest news!

Fact File
RADIO FACTS...

- All radio waves pick up interference as they travel through the air. When DAB broadcasts are decoded by a DAB radio, there is less interference.
- An improved technology known as DAB+ was introduced in 2008. DAB+ is almost three times more efficient, providing higher audio quality, even better reception and more stations.
- Digital radio is re-broadcast by cable and satellite TV companies so listeners can tune in with their televisions. Computer users can also listen to digital radio over the Internet.

Coolness Rating: 6/10

FUTURISTIC LIVING

21st Century Style

Futuristic homes use many clever energy-saving gadgets. Smart kitchens use low-energy appliances, and a smart shower keeps you clean and warm, while saving water.

Coolness Rating: 8/10

Fact File

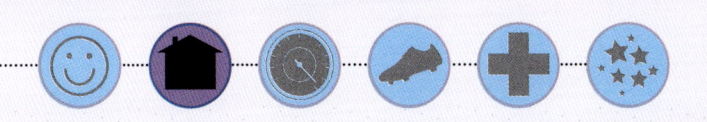

FUTURE LIVING FACTS...

- Smart fridge-freezers have a touch screen for TV and Internet. When items run out, you can re-order them online.
- With clever design, a kitchen can be made very small. It can even fold up against a wall!
- High-tech toilets respond at the touch of a button. Instead of toilet paper there's a fine spray with adjustable temperature and pressure. This is followed by warm air for drying.
- Toilet seat temperature can be controlled for comfort, and an air freshener is built in. There's even a radio and MP3 sound system to enjoy while you sit!

TOP GADGET

Bet you didn't know that...
- In a foldaway kitchen the hob and oven share heat.
- Water can be partly recycled.
- When the doors are closed, there's instant extra living space.

Did you know?
A shower uses about a third of the hot water needed to fill a bath, and it gets you cleaner.

ROBOTS

Helping Hands

Robots can do household chores while humans relax. They show off the latest in computer programs, speech recognition, sensors and motors.

Fact File

ROBOT FACTS...

- Robotic lawn mowers stay within a set area by sensing a magnetic field sent by a special wire boundary.
- Robots can be caring companions, especially for the elderly. They have webcam eyes and can speak about 10,000 words. If the owner does not respond after a certain time, they can call for help on a built-in mobile phone.
- Walking is very difficult for a robot. Scientists are developing better motion and balance sensors, and improved control programs and movement systems such as electric gears and motors.
- Some robot pet dogs can respond to more than 100 spoken commands, using speech-recognition technology.

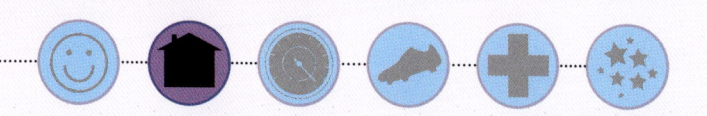

Coolness Rating: 10/10

Did you know?
'Robosapien' means robot toy designed to imitate human actions and movements.

TOP GADGET

Bet you didn't know that...
- The pool robot cleans your pool in about an hour.
- Roller brushes scrub tiled surfaces.
- A filtration system traps hair, debris and algae.
- Bumpers sense physical contact and steer away.

UNSCRAMBLE

Can you unscramble these gadget-related words?

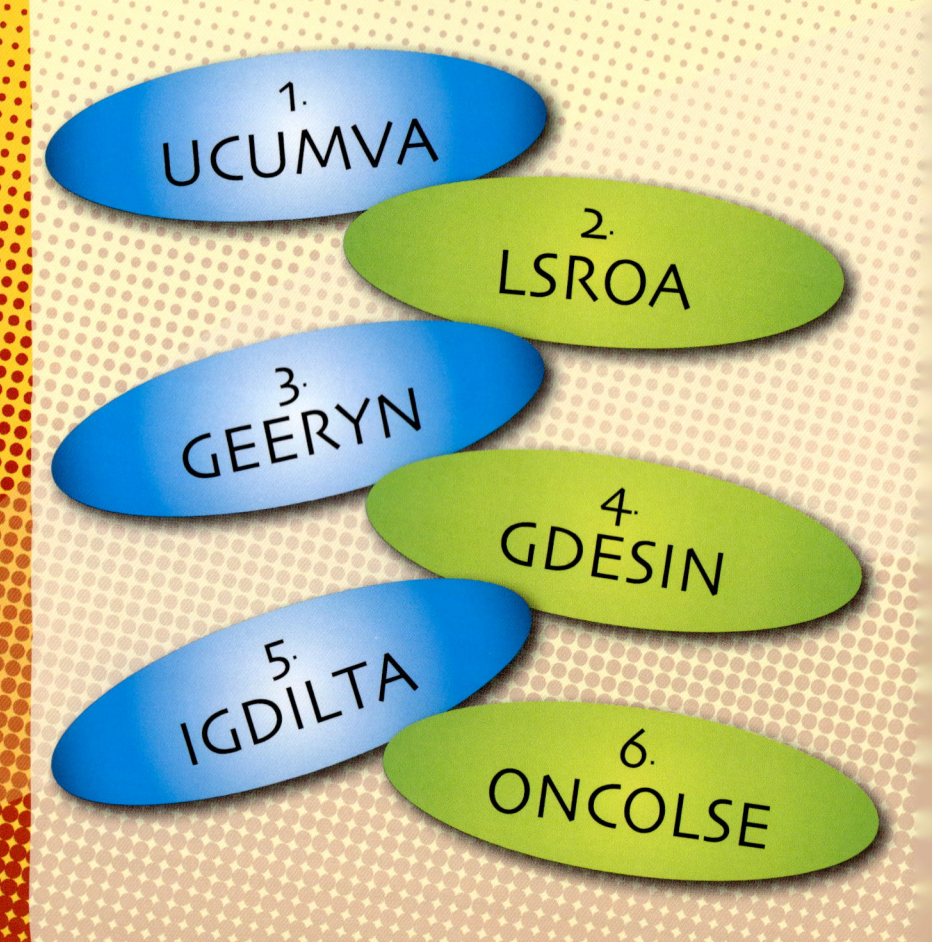

1. UCUMVA
2. LSROA
3. GEERYN
4. GDESIN
5. IGDILTA
6. ONCOLSE

7. BROOT

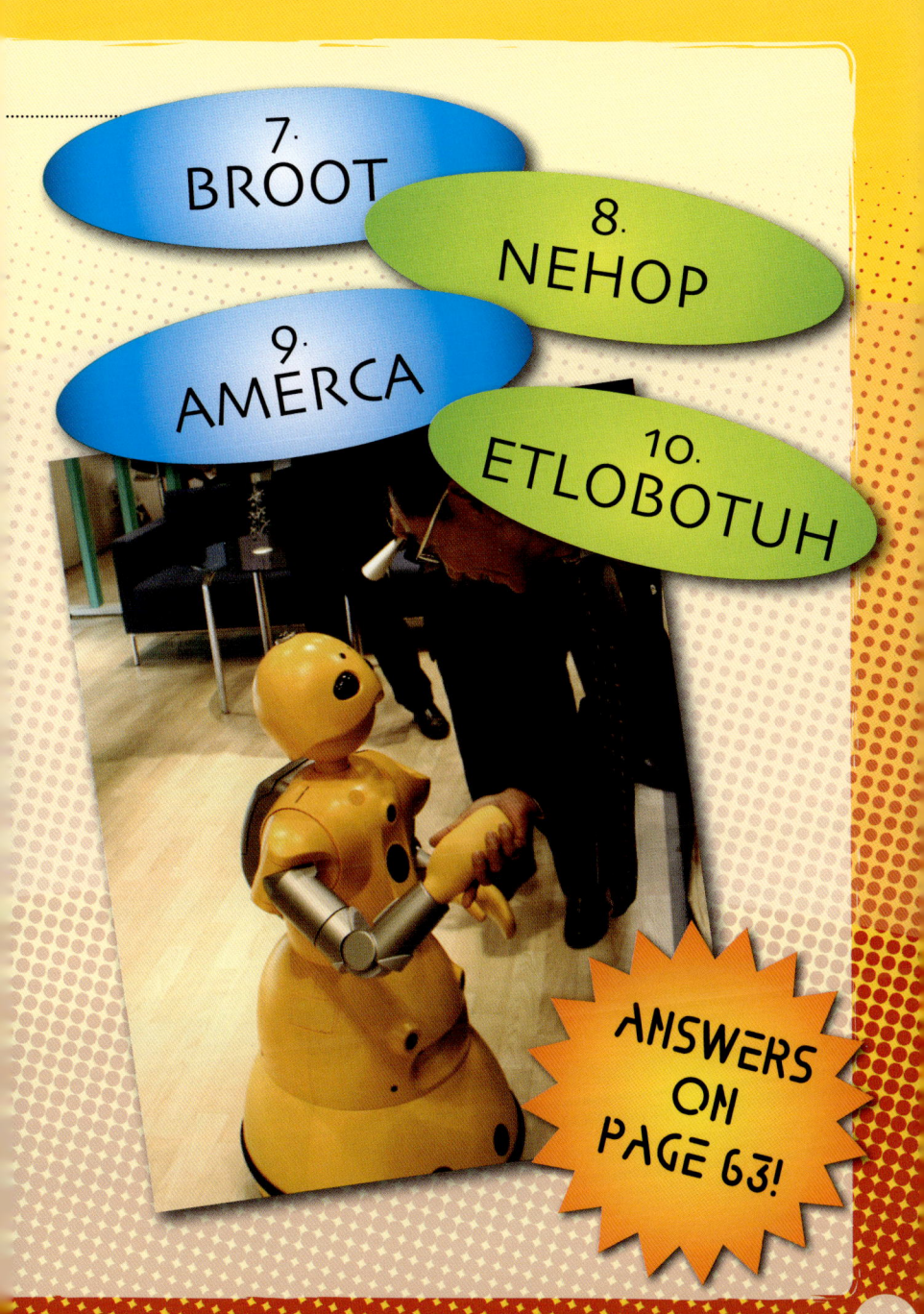

8. NEHOP

9. AMERCA

10. ETLOBOTUH

ANSWERS ON PAGE 63!

SPORTS CARS

Speed Demons

In 2005 the Bugatti Veyron 16.4 became the world's fastest, most powerful and most expensive road car.

TOP GADGET

Bet you didn't know that...
- Nuna is a series of solar-powered vehicles.
- The solar cells on Nuna cars change sunlight into electricity to run an electric motor.
- The Nuna 3 can achieve top speeds of 140 kph.

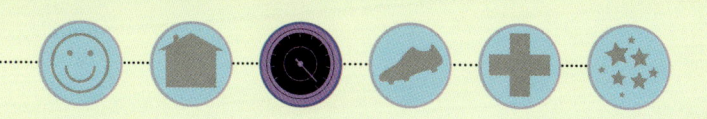

Did you know?

Veyrons can go from 0 to 100 kilometres per hour in less than 2.5 seconds, with a top speed of over 407 kilometres per hour.

Fact File

CAR FACTS...

- The standard V8 engine used in many super-fast cars has two rows of four cylinders at a 'V' angle to each other. The Veyron has two turbo-charged V8s partly merged together to make an eight-litre 'W16'!
- In a hydrogen fuel cell car, the electricity powers an electric motor to drive the wheels and run the car's systems.
- The Honda 2007 FCX's stack of fuel cells is about the size of a suitcase. It turns three-fifths of the energy in its hydrogen fuel into driving power. It gives out no polluting exhaust gases, makes very little noise, and the exhaust emissions are simply pure water.

Coolness Rating: 8/10

PRIVATE JETS

Luxury Life

Modern small passenger jets are packed with technology, from quiet and efficient engines to the latest satellite aids.

Fact File — JET FACTS...

- The Gulfstream 550 carries up to 18 passengers at a speed of 900 kilometres per hour and a height of 15,000 metres.
- On the flight deck, the captain sits on the left and the co-pilot on the right.
- Pulling back on the control column makes the plane rise, while tilting it to one side makes the plane lean.
- The private jet cabin has soft leather seats, plenty of legroom, individual tables and a luxurious toilet.
- Private jets are also used to bring home injured or sick people. They have hospital beds and specialist medical equipment on board.

Did you know?
A jet of hot gases spins exhaust turbines, then blasts out of the back, pushing the engine forwards.

Coolness Rating: 9/10

TOP GADGET

Bet you didn't know that...
New aircraft have small, turned-up winglets at the tips of the main wings. These create smooth airflow around the wingtips while reducing fuel usage and improving craft control.

POWER BOATS

Super Speed

The fastest power boats seem to 'fly', skimming from one wave to the next at 160 kilometres per hour.

Coolness Rating: 8/10

Wii

Canon
DIGITAL IXUS 75
CANON ZOOM LENS 3x
5.8-17.4mm 1:2.8-4.9
7.1 MEGA PIXELS

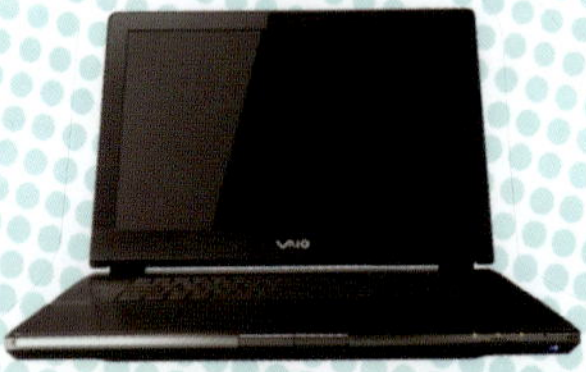
VAIO

SNAV

Logitech

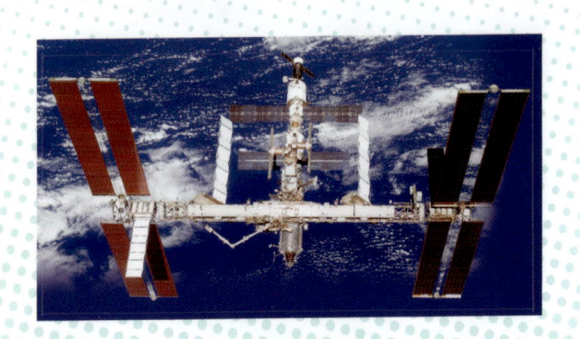

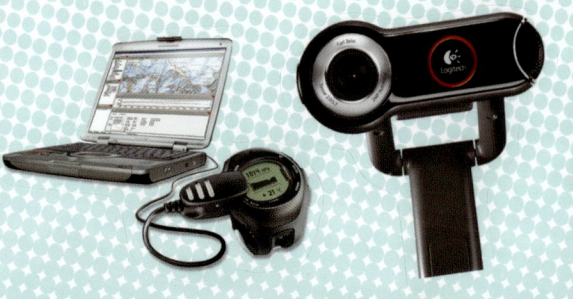

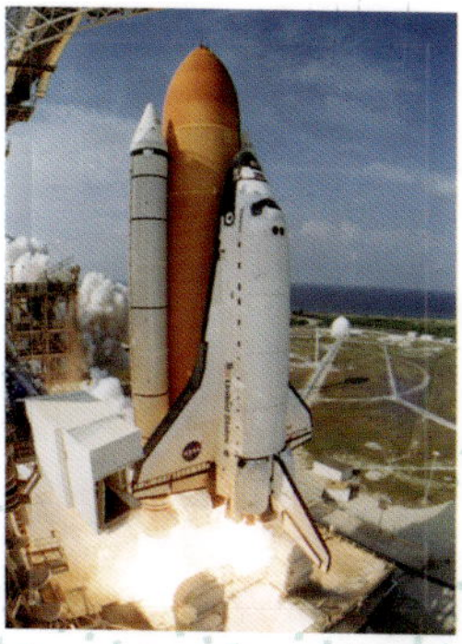

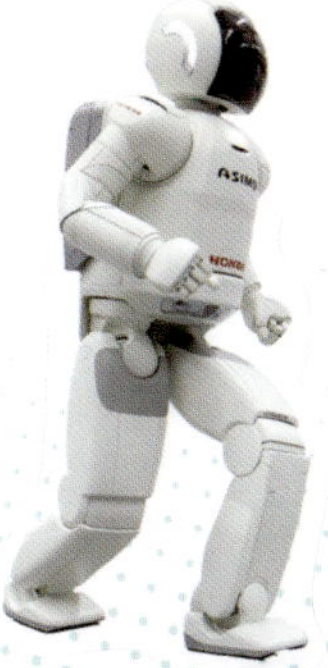

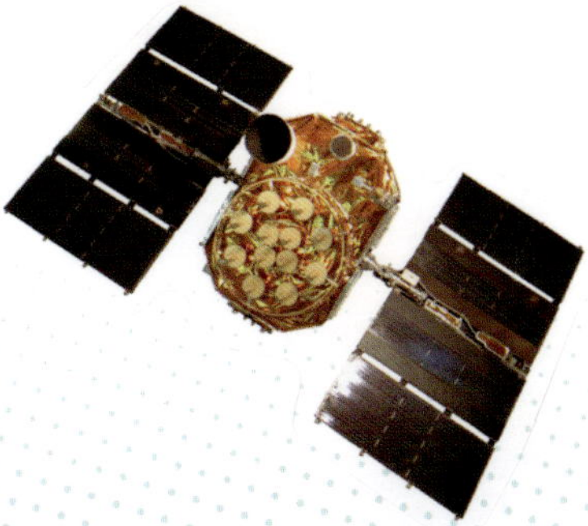

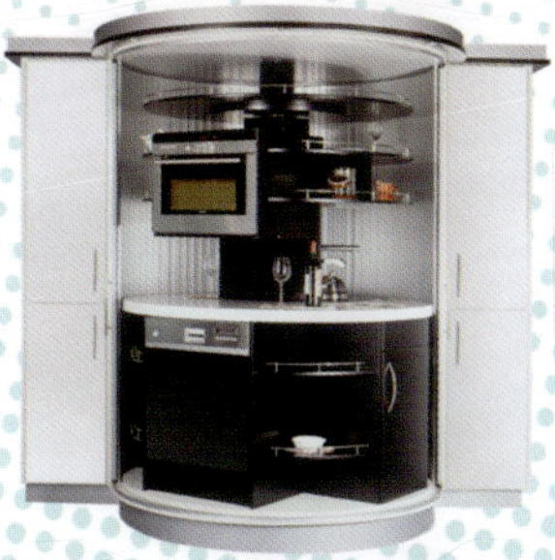

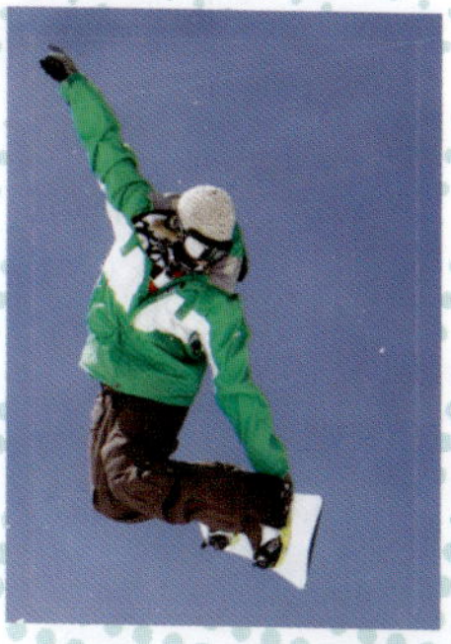

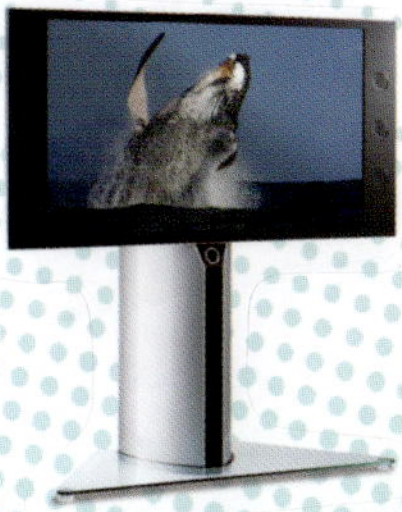

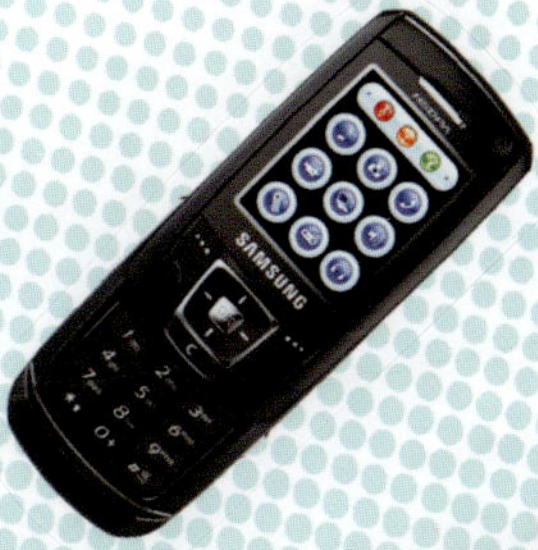
SAMSUNG

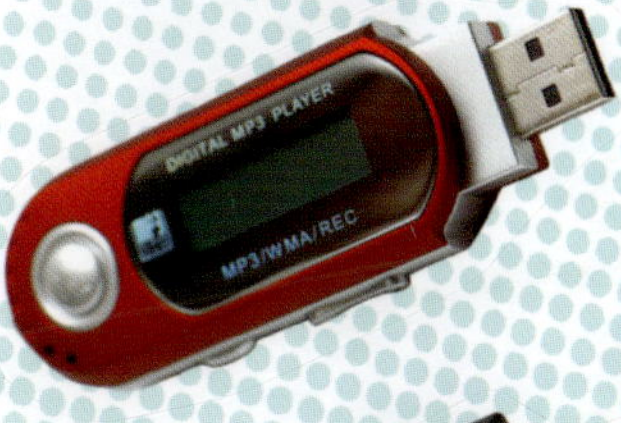
DIGITAL MP3 PLAYER
MP3/WMA/REC

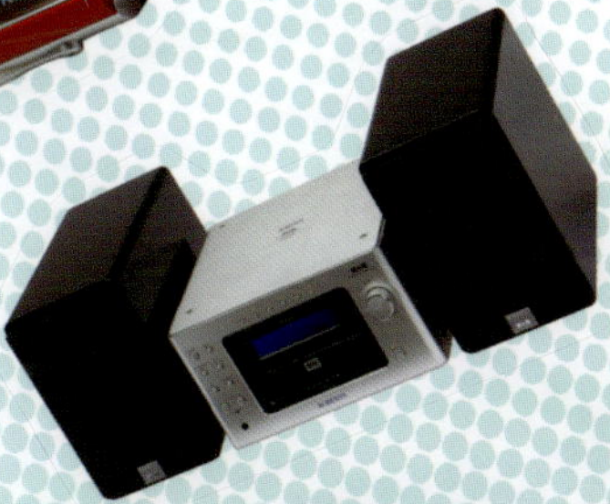

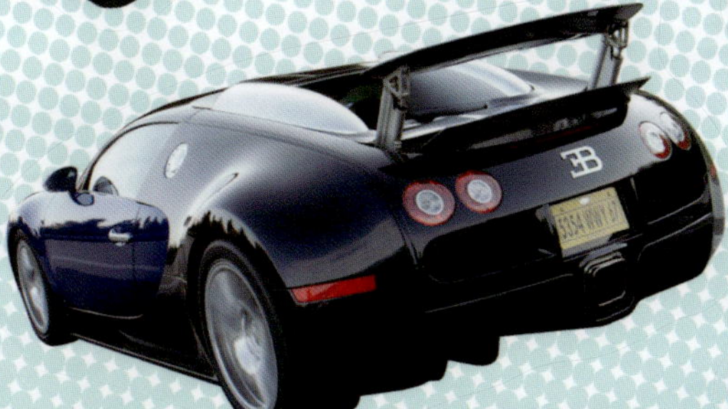

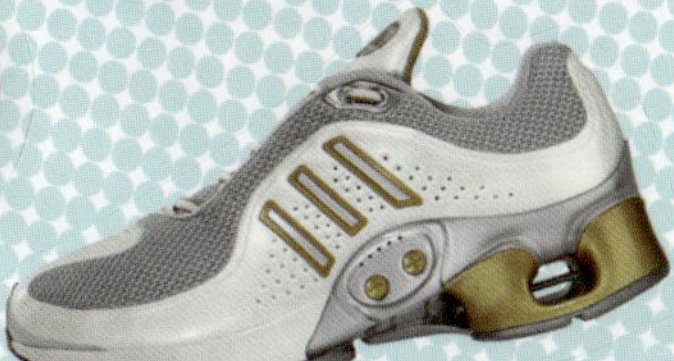

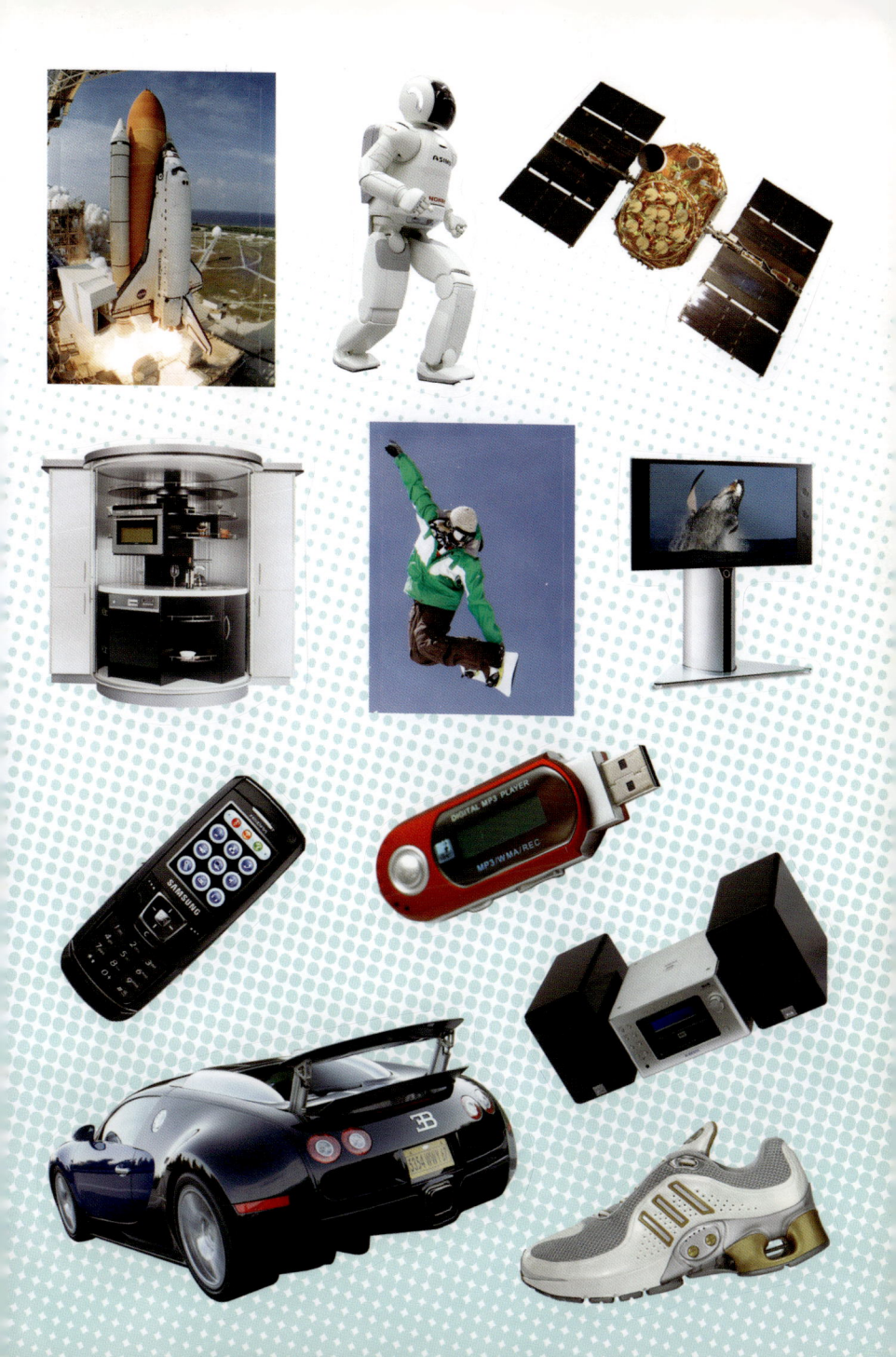

Fact File

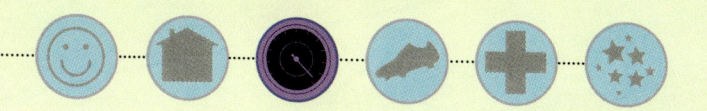

POWER BOAT FACTS...

- Power boats are designed to 'plane' across the water, which means that the boat's body, or hull, rises out of the water as it gains speed.
- The hull is built from fibreglass, which is light but tremendously strong, to withstand the hammer blows of smashing into the waves at high speed.
- Most power boats have marine diesel engines in the back. Instead of being cooled by air flowing past its radiator, the engine is cooled by water taken from the sea.

Did you know?

A power boat's propeller is designed to be half in and half out of the water.

TOP GADGET

Bet you didn't know that...

- P1 power boats are the sea's version of F1 (Formula One) racing cars.
- Their total engine size must be less than 11 litres. That's five times larger than a family car engine!

SATNAV

Perfect Positioning

Small satnav (satellite navigation) devices in cars, watches and even mobiles can receive signals from GPS (Global Positioning System) satellites to pinpoint your location anywhere on Earth.

Coolness Rating: 9/10

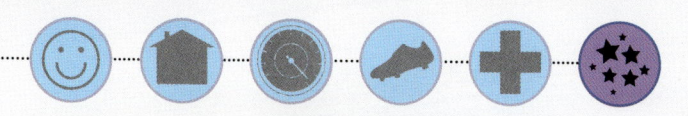

TOP GADGET

Bet you didn't know that...
- There are more than 30 Navstar satellites in the GPS. They are arranged in six main groups.
- Satellites follow each other round and round the Earth.

Did you know?
Each satellite is about 20,200 kilometres up, travels at 14,000 kilometres per hour and makes two orbits every 24 hours.

Fact File — SATELLITE FACTS...

- The positions of GPS satellites mean that signals from up to six satellites can be received anywhere on Earth.
- Each GPS satellite sends out radio signals about its own identity code, its precise position, and the exact time. The GPS receiver compares the time delays from each of the satellites to find its distance from them, and so its own position.
- A pocket satnav receiver may have a touch-screen that allows you to pinpoint your exact location. It also shows routes and times between locations.
- Athletes use GPS watches to record how far and how fast they run.

35

MATCHING SENTENCES

The sentences below are all missing a word. Choose from the three words below each sentence to complete it.

1. The _____ in a hydrogen fuel cell car powers an electric motor.

petrol *diesel* *electricity*

2. Some private jets have hospital beds and _____ equipment on board.

swimming *school* *medical*

3. The engines of P1 power boats are about _____ times larger than a family car engine.

five *20,200* *24*

4. Many new aircraft have small, turned-up _____ at the tips of the main wings.

- quads
- winglets
- fish

5. Marine diesel engines are cooled by _____ water.

- shallow
- sea
- hot

ANSWERS ON PAGE 63!

SNOW AND SURF GADGETS

Brilliant Boards

As scientists invent new materials for other uses, such as in cars or rockets, these inventions find their way to surfboard and snowboard makers.

Did you know?

A snowboard is heavier at the front than at the back. It must bend easily and flex in different directions.

Coolness Rating: 10/10

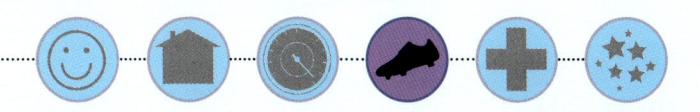

TOP GADGET

Bet you didn't know that...
- Surfboards are made from a large slab of plastic-like foam called a blank.
- The board is covered with fibreglass material and epoxy resin glue, which sets hard and smooth.

Fact File — SNOWBOARDING FACTS...

- Boots are fixed to a snowboard with straps called bindings.
- Bindings hold the feet in a well-balanced position.
- A shorter board enables better jumping and twisting.
- A snowboarder gets to know exactly how the board will twist and slide by feeling its movements through their feet.
- Snowboarding trousers have reinforced knees and seats.

RACING GADGETS

Cool Competing

There are many types of racing vehicles, including sports cars, mountain bikes and superbikes.

Fact File

RACING FACTS...

- A superbike's tyres have a wrap-around tread (the pattern of grooves). This means the tyre still grips as the rider leans at a low angle around a bend.
- A mountain bike computer can calculate the distance travelled, and average and fastest speeds. Some bike computers now also have GPS systems.
- An F1 car comes into the pits two or three times during a race. The heavy fuel hose delivers 12 litres per second. Damaged body panels are replaced, and the driver's helmet visor is cleaned.

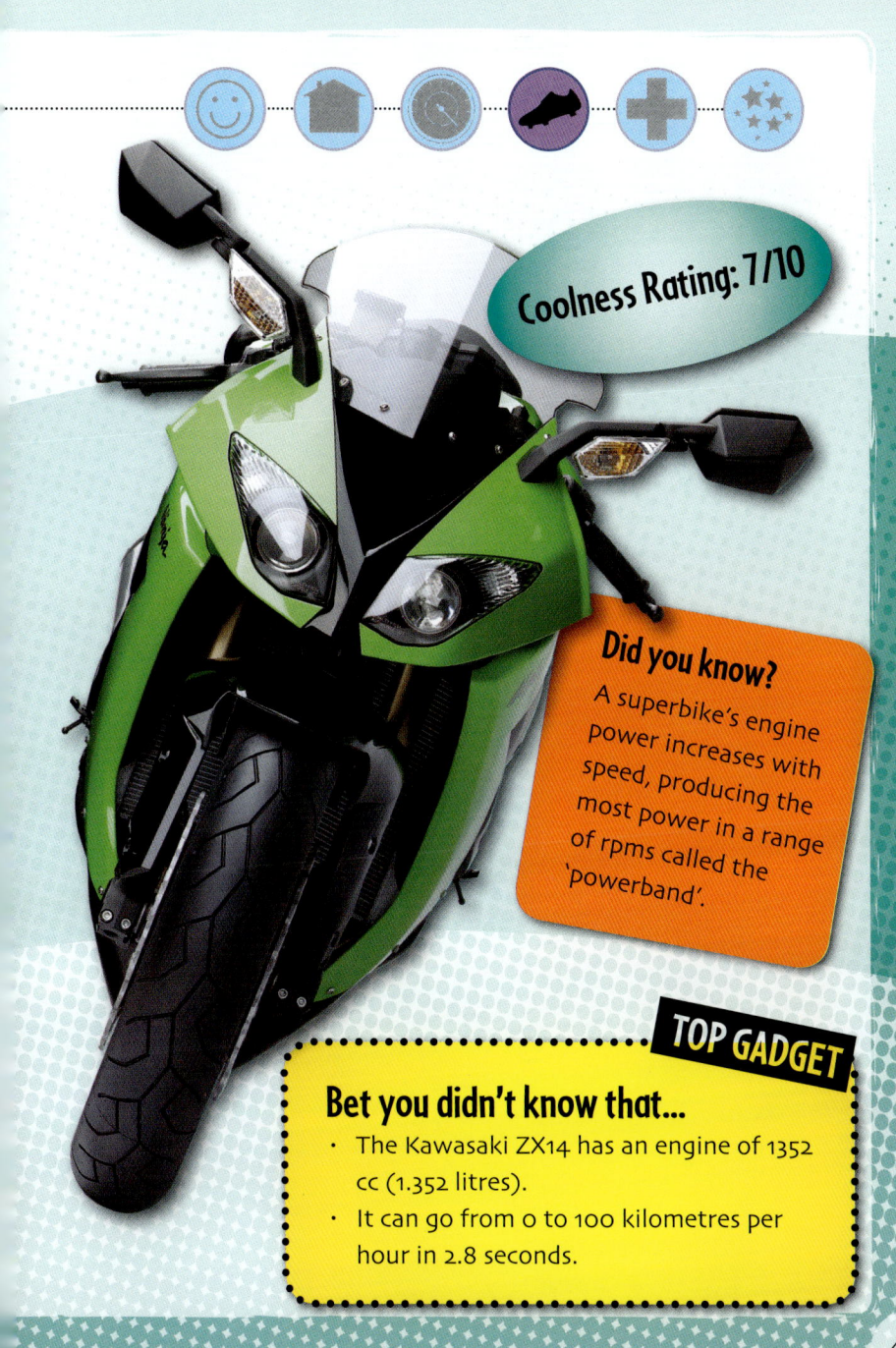

Coolness Rating: 7/10

Did you know?
A superbike's engine power increases with speed, producing the most power in a range of rpms called the 'powerband'.

TOP GADGET

Bet you didn't know that...
- The Kawasaki ZX14 has an engine of 1352 cc (1.352 litres).
- It can go from 0 to 100 kilometres per hour in 2.8 seconds.

TRAINERS TECHNOLOGY

Fancy Footwear

There are hundreds of specially designed sports trainers and boots, each made for a particular activity.

Coolness Rating: 5/10

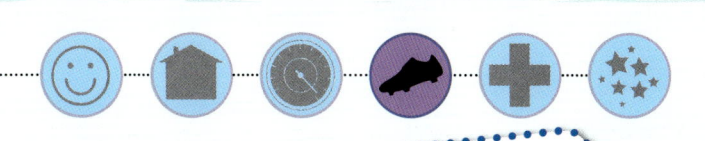

Fact File

FOOTWEAR FACTS...

- Players of football, rugby, cricket and similar sports have to cope with many different ground conditions. They change their studs to suit the conditions.
- Studs fit into sockets in the soles. They can be varied to give more grip to the ball of the foot and less at the tip and heel.

Did you know?

Football boot studs are usually long for soft ground, so they stick in more and grip better.

TOP GADGET

Bet you didn't know that...

The Adidas 1 trainer has a special heel sensor which:
- Records a thousand changes in pressure each second.
- Sends the information to a microchip that controls a small electric motor.
- Turns a screw that changes the cushioning in the heel.

WRIST GADGETS

Wacky Watches

The latest wristwatch computers can display your exact geographical position, altitude, depth or speed. They can even forecast the weather!

Fact File — WATCH FACTS...

- The Suunto watch display shows time, altitude and a stopwatch.
- The watch includes a compass, altimeter and barometer, and has its own storm alarm.
- The casing is water-resistant to depths of 100 metres.
- The lightweight GPS Pod clips onto your belt or jacket. It uses GPS to track speed and distance.

Did you know?
A laptop computer can download your watch's information and display a map to show the route it took.

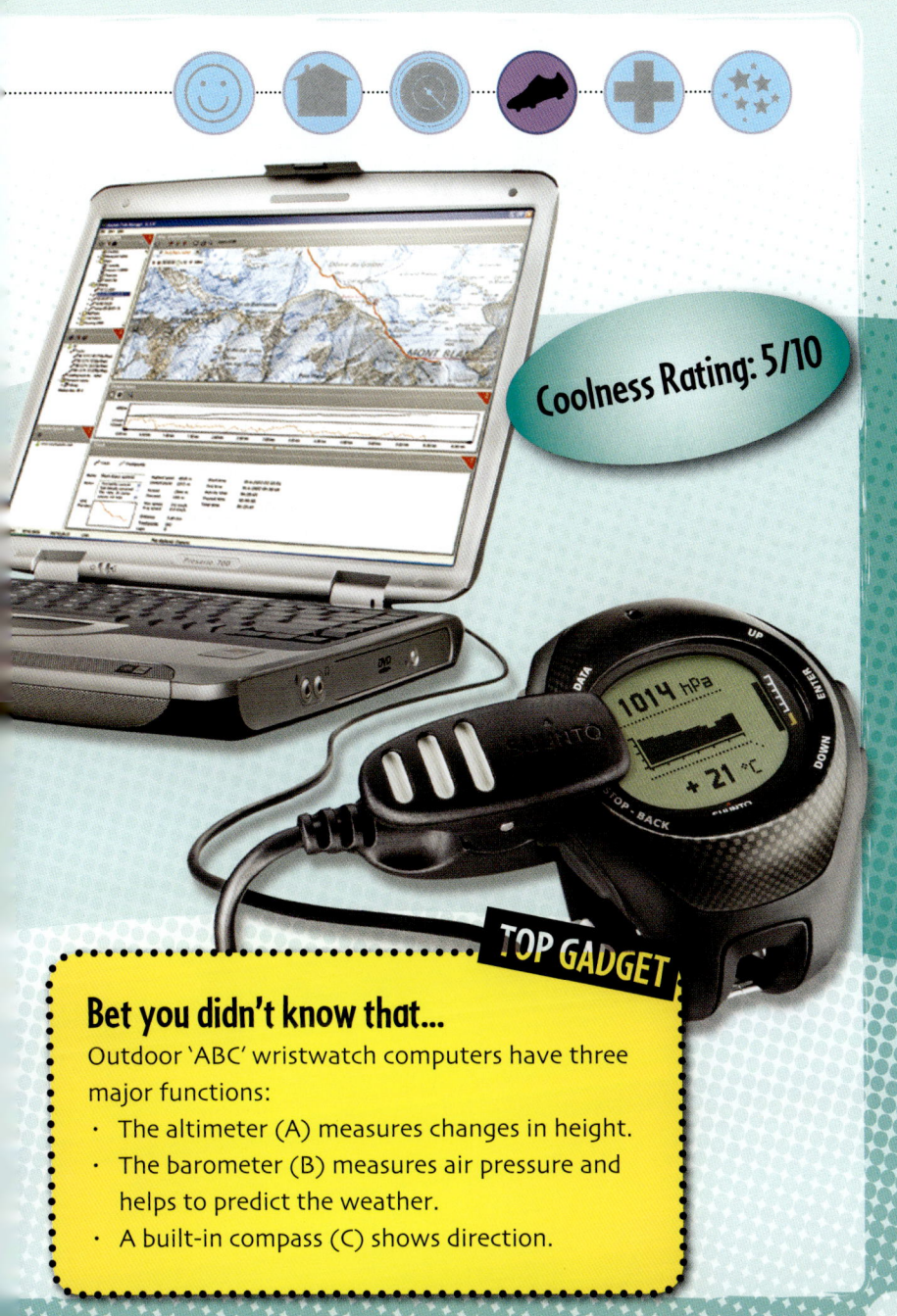

Coolness Rating: 5/10

TOP GADGET

Bet you didn't know that...
Outdoor 'ABC' wristwatch computers have three major functions:
- The altimeter (A) measures changes in height.
- The barometer (B) measures air pressure and helps to predict the weather.
- A built-in compass (C) shows direction.

45

AMAZING MACHINES QUIZ

1. What is the Bugatti Veyron's top speed?
   a) 207 kph
   b) 407 kph
   c) 607 kph

2. How high can the Gulfstream 550 jet fly?
   a) 9000 metres
   b) 900 metres
   c) 15,000 metres

3. What speed can a power boat travel at?
   a) 160 kph
   b) 120 kph
   c) 80 kph

4. How long does it take the Kawasaki ZX14 to go from 0 to 100 kph?
   a) 2.8 seconds
   b) 4.7 seconds
   c) 6.6 seconds

5. What is the hull of a power boat made from?
   a) Polyurethane
   b) Wood
   c) Fibreglass

ANSWERS ON PAGE 63!

47

SCANNERS

Top Technology

Modern medicine is at the cutting edge of science. Scanners take 'snapshots' of the insides of our bodies and can take several images each second, like a movie, to show how our insides work.

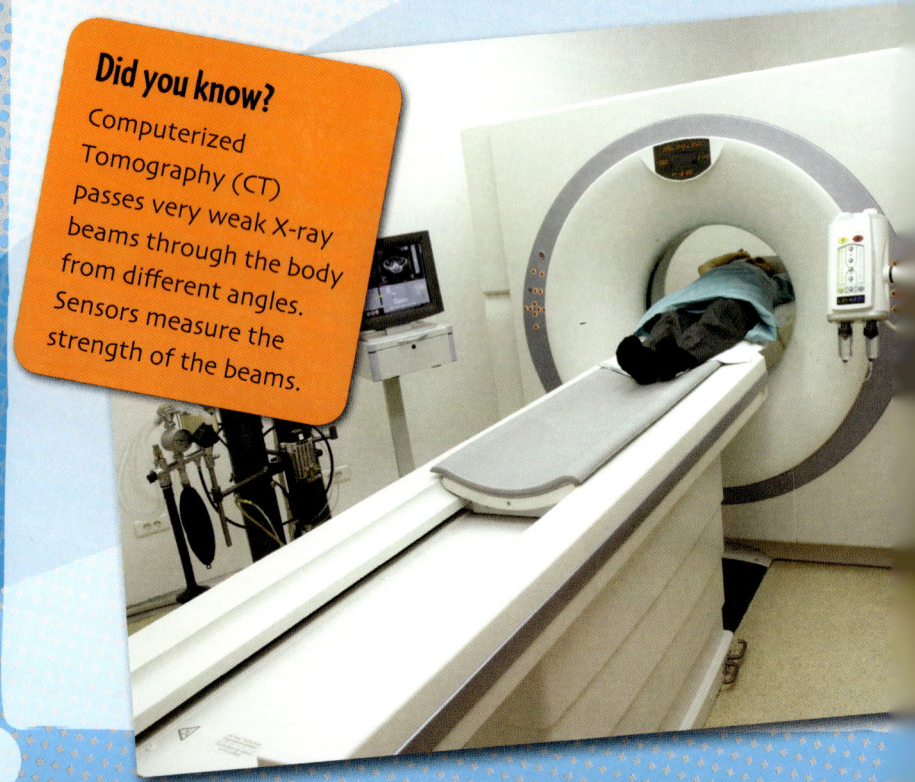

Did you know?
Computerized Tomography (CT) passes very weak X-ray beams through the body from different angles. Sensors measure the strength of the beams.

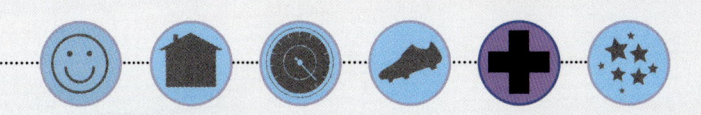

Coolness Rating: 8/10

TOP GADGET

Bet you didn't know that...

- In Magnetic Resonance Imaging (MRI), a very strong magnetic field makes hydrogen atoms in the body line up.
- A radio wave knocks the atoms out of line.
- As they line up again, they send out weak radio signals.
- The scanner uses these signals to build images of the body.

Fact File — SCANNER FACTS...

- A plain X-ray image is like a photograph of the body. It shows hard, dense parts, such as bones and teeth, as white areas. It does not reveal soft tissues such as muscles.
- Scanners such as CT and MRI take a series of images like 'slices' through the body. A computer then puts them together to produce a 3-D image of the body part.
- Ultrasound scanners send harmless, very high-pitched sound waves into the body, and measure how these bounce back off different parts.

49

MEDICAL CAMERAS

Surgical Snapshots

Some of the world's smallest cameras can be swallowed in a capsule or inserted into the body on the end of a gadget called an endoscope.

Fact File ENDOSCOPE FACTS...

- The camera in an endoscope focuses light through the lens and along a bundle of optical fibres to the eyepiece. Each fibre carries light from a tiny part of the view.
- To guide an endoscope inside a patient's body, the surgeon operates the handle to pull thin wires within the cable's length. The cable can twist around corners and loop back on itself.
- There is usually a hollow channel in the tip of the cable for sucking up samples of body fluids. There may also be tiny pincers to grab a sample of tissue, or a blade to cut away a problem like a blood clot.

Coolness Rating: 8/10

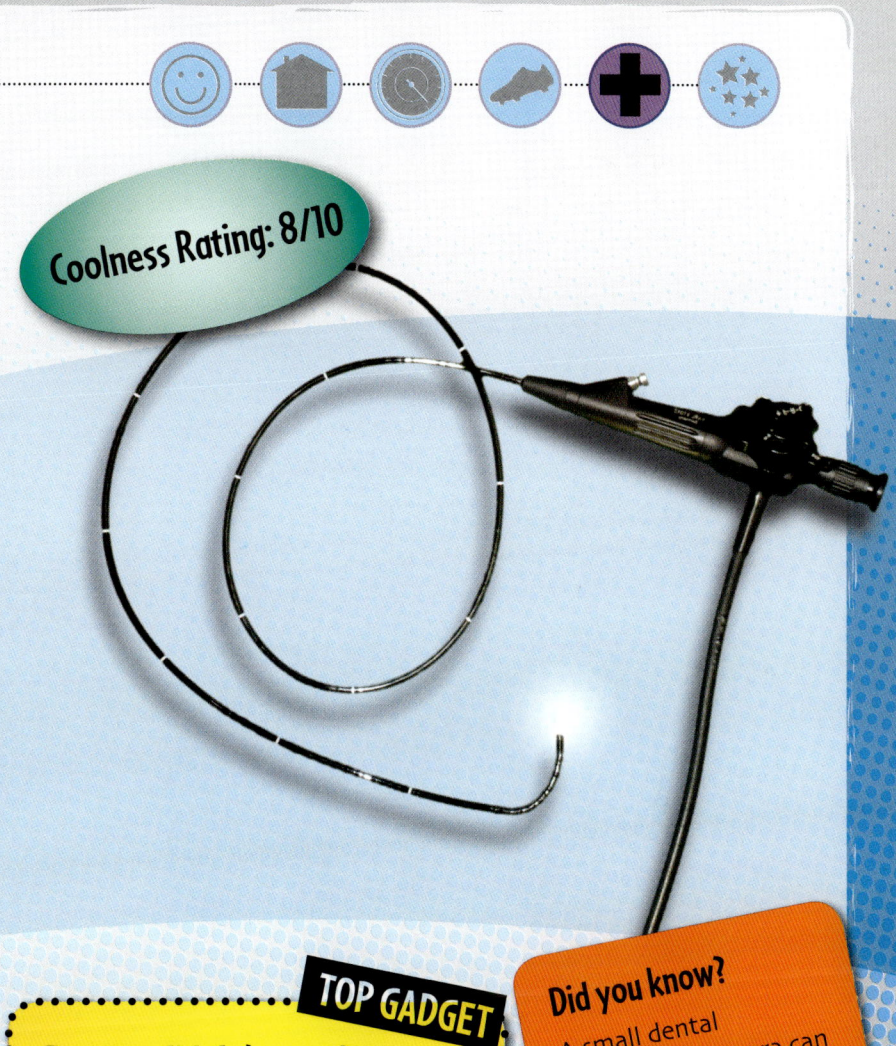

TOP GADGET

Bet you didn't know that...
- A capsule camera is swallowed by the patient.
- It can spot problems with the stomach or intestines.

Did you know?
A small dental magnifying camera can get into all corners of the mouth, and shows an enlarged view on a screen.

MEDICAL ROBOTS

Droid Doctors

Some operations are so tricky that only a few specialist surgeons can do them. But if the surgeon and patient are half a world apart, they can use a robot surgeon.

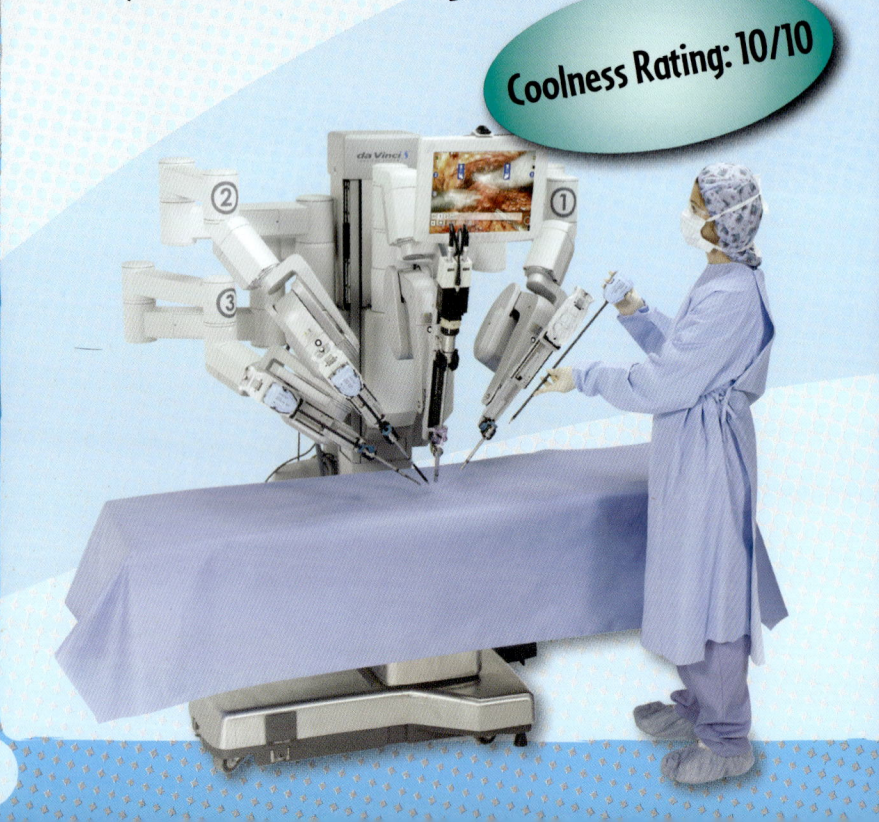

Coolness Rating: 10/10

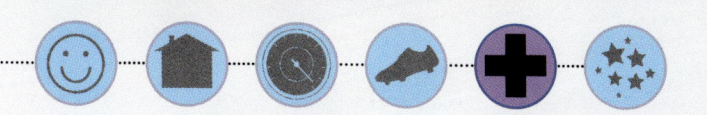

Fact File

ROBOT SURGEON FACTS...

- The surgeon's EndoWrist console contains two sets of control mechanisms with multiple levers and joints that can move in all directions. These movements are then coded into signals, which are sent to the robot surgeon to copy.
- The surgeon watches the operation on special 3-D goggles. Foot pedals control the cameras so the surgeon can make the view zoom in or out, or move left, right, up or down.
- Future medical 'nanobots' could be small enough to float in the blood and even get into body cells.
- Some microscopic germs, such as those that cause malaria, hide and multiply inside red blood cells. Medical nanobots could find and destroy the infected red cells and their germs.

Did you know?

The robot surgeon has four or more sets of 'hands' with detachable tips.

TOP GADGET

Bet you didn't know that...

- Nanoscale robots could detect blood clots and break them apart if they were dangerous.
- Nanocapsules could contain tiny amounts of medicine that they release only when they get to the body part that needs the treatment.

IMAGE RECOGNITION

Can you tell what's in the pictures below? Write the name of the object next to each picture and then check your answers!

1. _____

2. _____

3. _____

4. _____

5. _____

6. _____

ANSWERS ON PAGE 63!

55

ROCKETS AND LAUNCHERS

Blast Off!

In 1969, the first humans reached the Moon on the USA's Apollo 11. Today, spacecraft travel to the edges of our solar system, satellites chase comets and shuttles take astronauts to work on the International Space Station.

Coolness Rating: 10/10

TOP GADGET

Bet you didn't know that...
- Europe's main launchers are Ariane rockets.
- Two boosters help during the first two minutes of flight.
- The boosters detach and parachute into the sea.
- They are reused in the next mission.

Did you know?
As a rocket engine burns fuel, hot gases roar downwards. This force pushes the engine up, carrying the rocket with it.

Fact File — ROCKET FACTS...

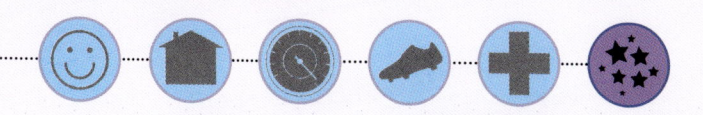

- All space launch vehicles are powered by rockets. A rocket burns fuel to make a blast of hot gases, which carry it upwards.
- A payload is what a rocket carries into space. It could be a satellite to orbit Earth, a probe that heads into deep space, a crew of astronauts or parts for a space station.
- Most rockets cannot be used more than once. All four parts of the space shuttle can be re-used. The massive fuel tanks are jettisoned but then recovered from the sea.

INTERNATIONAL SPACE STATION

Orbiting HQ

Since 1998, the International Space Station (ISS) has gradually been built from parts carried into space by space shuttles and launchers.

Did you know?
A space-lift cable would have to be 35,780 kilometres long.

Coolness Rating: 8/10

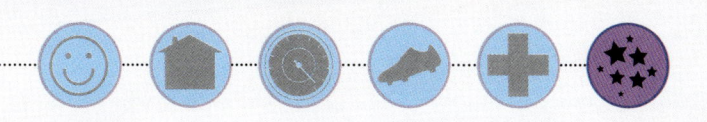

Fact File

SPACE STATION FACTS...

- The ISS moves at almost 8 metres per second, orbiting Earth nearly 16 times each day. Visiting spacecraft make airtight attachments to it at the docking ports.
- Because it is in orbit, the ISS is constantly 'falling' in a circle. Inside, everything is weightless and floats about if not fixed down.
- An astronaut's body is also weightless in space. Being weightless means the body's muscles have no gravity to work against, so they weaken. Astronauts have regular work-outs on exercise machines.
- The life support technology in the ISS is vital for survival. Electric heaters provide warmth. The air is filtered and recycled, with vital oxygen added. All the water, including washing water and urine, must be recycled and purified.

TOP GADGET

Bet you didn't know that...

One idea for doing away with rockets is to have a space lift. A long cable would extend from Earth's surface far into space. Climber devices would crawl up the cable, taking satellites, space probes and parts for space stations.

SATELLITES

Galaxy-Goers

Artificial satellites are devices designed to orbit Earth, the Sun, the Moon or another planet. They are used for communication or to transmit scientific data back to Earth.

Fact File

SATELLITE FACTS...

- Satellite Swift is 6 metres long, weighs 1.5 tonnes, and orbits the Earth 600 kilometres high every 90 minutes.
- Satellite Stereo is not one satellite but two. Like the Earth, they orbit the Sun, with Stereo A more than a million kilometres ahead of our planet, and Stereo B a similar distance behind.
- The two Stereos take images at the same time from millions of kilometres apart. Computers combine these into one 3-D picture that gives much more information than a 2-D image.

Coolness Rating: 8/10

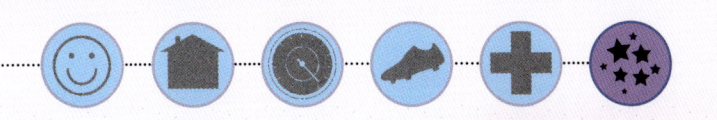

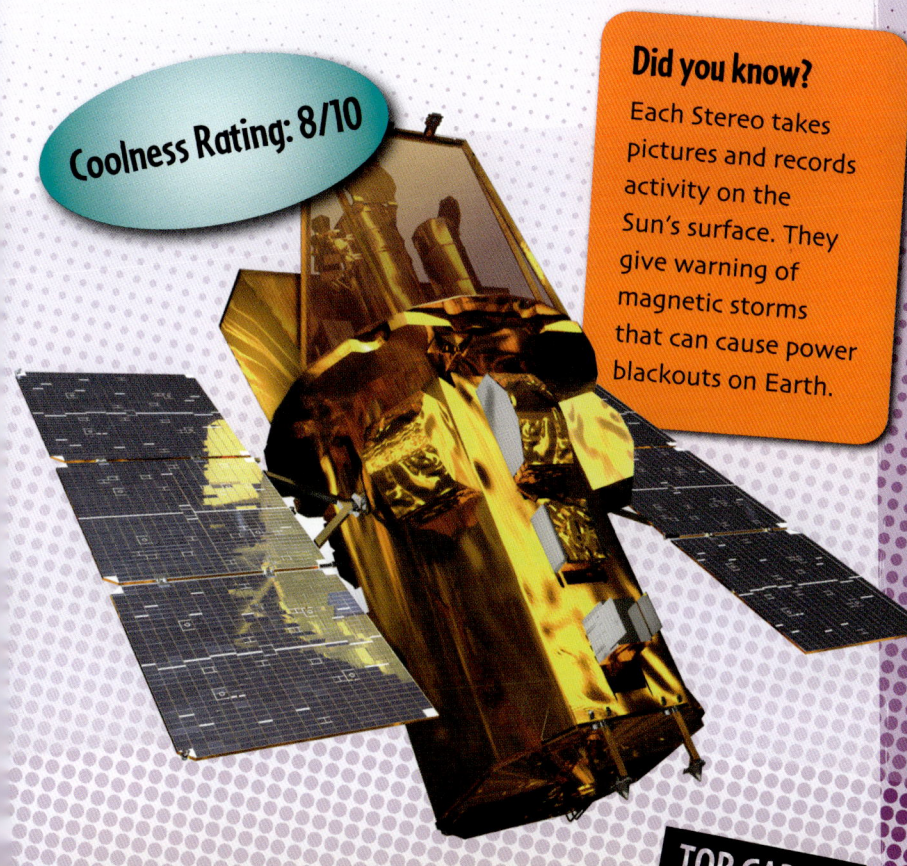

Did you know?
Each Stereo takes pictures and records activity on the Sun's surface. They give warning of magnetic storms that can cause power blackouts on Earth.

TOP GADGET

Bet you didn't know that...
- Swift was sent to study mysterious gamma-ray bursts (GRBs).
- GRBs are the most powerful explosions in the Universe.
- It is thought they are caused by the collapse or collision of massive stars.

61

INDEX

BlackBerry 15
Bluetooth 17
Bugatti Veyron 28, 29

cameras 10-11, 14, 17, 19, 50-1
capsule camera 51
cinemas 13
computers 15, 16-17, 19, 40, 44, 49
CT (Computerised Tomography) 48

DAB (Digital Audio Broadcasting) 20, 21
dental magnifying camera 51
digital cameras 10-11, 14, 17, 19
digital radio 20-1

email 14, 15
endoscope 50

fridge-freezers 23
fuel cell cars 29

games consoles 8-9
GPS (Global Positioning System) 34-5, 40, 44
GPS watches 35
GRBs (gamma-ray bursts) 61

HDTV 12

IMAX cinemas 13
International Space Station 56, 58-9
internet 14, 18-19, 21

jet aircraft 30-1

laptops 16-17, 44
lawn mowers 24
liquid crystal technology 12, 15

medical gadgets 48-53
memory cards and sticks 17
mobile phones 9, 14-15
mountain bikes 40
MP3 player 6-7, 9
MP4 watch 6, 9
MRI (Magnetic Resonance Imaging) 49

nanobots 53
nanocapsules 53

PDAs (personal digital assistants) 15
plasma screens 12
pool robots 25
power boats 32-3

robosapiens 25
robot surgeons 52-3
robots 24-5, 52-3
rockets and launchers 56-7, 58